Love in the 90s

Love in the 90s

B.B. & Jo · The Story of a Lifelong Love

A Granddaughter's Portrait by Keri Pickett

WARNER BOOKS

A Time Warner Company

DEVELOPED AND PRODUCED BY

BURLINGTON, VERMONT
GARY CHASSMAN & JULIE STILLMAN

DESIGN · ROBERT A. YERKS
EDITORIAL ASSISTANCE · BRIGITTE FRASE

WARNER BOOKS, INC.
1271 AVENUE OF THE AMERICAS · NEW YORK, NY 10020

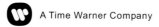 A Time Warner Company

PRINTED IN HONG KONG BY PALACE PRESS INTERNATIONAL
FIRST PRINTING: NOVEMBER 1995
10 9 8 7 6 5 4 3 2 1
ISBN 0-446-52032-2
LC 95-61153

ALL CONTEMPORARY PHOTOGRAPHS BY
KERI PICKETT

INFORMATION ABOUT PRINTS
OF PHOTOGRAPHS IN THIS BOOK
CAN BE OBTAINED THROUGH:

KERI PICKETT PHOTOGRAPHY
413 EAST HENNEPIN AVENUE
MINNEAPOLIS, MN 55414-1005
E-MAIL: BB and JO
AT AMERICA ONLINE

INFORMATION ABOUT THE
SUBSEQUENT USE OF THESE
AND OTHER PHOTOGRAPHS
CAN BE OBTAINED THROUGH:

SWANSTOCK
P.O. BOX 2350
TUCSON, AZ 85702
602-622-7133

This book is dedicated to my family
for providing an environment where hugging and kissing and saying I love you
are as natural a part of life as breathing.

INTRODUCTION

*T*his book is the portrait, in photographs and letters, of a relationship that remained an abiding romance and a deeply affectionate friendship for sixty-four years. My grandparents' letters reveal the development of their life-partnership, and my photographs show the deeply caring and intimate relationship they continued to share at the end of their life together.

B.B. and Jo's courtship and love story are part of my family folk history. Their devotion to each other was both unique and universal. They are all of us. We yearn to love and to be loved. We all want our thoughts and our needs to be acknowledged by someone who cares. The love that B.B. and Jo shared shows a commitment that we all search for throughout our lives, and few of us are fortunate enough to find. My grandparents always said their only disagreement was who got the better end of the deal.

I didn't set out to do a book. I was just spending time with Grandma and Grandpa because I love them deeply. As long as I had my camera, I would shoot a few frames at the end of a roll of film. The photographs in this book were made when my grandparents were in their mid-nineties and I was in my early thirties; the letters were written nearly seventy years ago. I have also included many old family photographs to illuminate and deepen the appreciation of the letters. I have woven the photographs and letters together in the hope that they will provide others with the same inspiration and understanding I have received from my grandparents' extraordinary relationship.

THE STORY OF B.B. AND JO

Bernard Buckner Blakey was born on February 22, 1895, on a farm near Maude, Missouri. He came from a family of eight children, who were orphaned when he was seven years old. The four older children took care of the younger ones: Marcus took Leon, Roy took John, Anna took Bernard, and Susan took Lois. The Blakeys were a family of educated people who went on to distinguish themselves in their respective fields.

Josie Lou Lydia Walker Blakey was born on December 17, 1896, in Indian Territory, which later became the forty-sixth state, Oklahoma. Her family was poor — she remembers picking a hundred pounds of cotton a day as a child, and playing with dolls made out of corncobs. She is very proud to have grown up among the Cherokees, and to have been friend and neighbor to Will Rogers' aunt and uncle. Josie was one of eleven children. Members of her family did not go beyond required schooling, and her father saw no reason for a girl to go beyond the eighth grade. But with the help of her brother Fred, she completed high school, and with the aid of her cousins, Adeline and Clifford Shirley, she went on to college.

"I was thirty-two before I married. Most girls were married by eighteen, and you were considered an old maid if you were not," Grandma says. When she and Grandpa met, she had graduated from Phillips University, a church-affiliated college in Enid, Oklahoma. Upon graduation, Josie was ordained as a minister in the Disciples of Christ denomination. She traveled a fifteen-state region by train, setting up church schools and religious education programs.

Grandpa was thirty-four when he married Grandma. He had graduated from the University of Minnesota in 1922 and was running a hardware business with his brother Leon (A.L.) in Tulsa, Oklahoma.

"First time I met Josie," B.B. said, "I had just broken off my engagement with Ione Manrose and then was sorry I had. I tried to put it back together again, but Ione wouldn't have it." B.B. went to Enid from Tulsa, hoping to find Ione Manrose at the home of the Shirleys, but when he called there, it was Josephine Walker who answered the door.

Josie began an occasional correspondence with B.B., trying to reunite him with Ione. He became interested in Josie instead. "I didn't know that I was impressing him the way I was," she told me, "but I thought he was a really nice gentleman, and that Ione and he were having really unnecessary trouble and I was going to fix it up."

Grandma moved to a new post in Kentucky and the preacher there became interested in her. To discourage him, she asked Grandpa to write her pretending to be her beau. What followed was a year-long exchange of letters through which they got to know each other and fell in love.

They were married on July 14, 1929. Grandma became pregnant three months later, but she continued to work during the first couple years of their marriage. Grandpa and his brother A.L. lost their hardware store in the Depression. Josie took over B.B.'s position as church director, and he tried selling life insurance, but the country was broke and no one was buying. Eventually, he was asked to work in the business office at Phillips University, and many years later Grandma became the official hostess to the student center.

When we were cleaning out my grandparents' home after Grandpa's death, I found a small envelope marked "censored." Inside there were pictures of B.B. with some of his old girlfriends.

B.B. and Jo had three children: Roy Blakey, Marian Blakey Spencer, and my mother, Berna Jo (B.J.) Blakey French. My sister, Kim Mahling Clark, and I are their only grandchildren.

Grandpa died on February 24, 1992, in Minneapolis, Minnesota, at the age of ninety-seven. After he died, I finally looked into the big box of love letters they had saved and, reading them, watched their story unfold and come to life. The letters lay a foundation for their life together. They always maintained their delightfully romantic and upbeat attitude about life. They never walked down the hall without her arm through his. They never lost their love for books. She always laughed at his jokes. He couldn't sit next to her without touching her. They were frequently mistaken for honeymooners.

After his death, I asked Grandma a personal question I wasn't sure she would answer. "How old were you when you and Grandpa stopped making love?" "We never stopped making it!" she said. "We made it up to the very end. I remember our honeymoon. He wanted to spare me, but I had waited thirty-two years and I wasn't going to let him keep it." Later, I told Grandma that my mother was uncomfortable having that story made public. Grandma thought about it and said, "Well, the book would need to have some sex in it or it wouldn't be natural."

Taken together, these letters and photographs show the beginning and end of a lifelong love. The love B.B. and Jo shared says so much about what is possible for us all.

A Love Story Told In Letters And Photographs

Grandpa fell in love with Grandma when she was trying to deflect the attentions of a preacher in Kentucky, who had invited her to supervise an education program in his church. She asked Grandpa to write pretending to be "her friend." That started a daily, year-long correspondence, resulting in a treasure of over 700 letters.

Dear Blakey,

I arrived here Monday afternoon and have been quite busy every hour since, having conferences with teachers and getting ready for the school. I am about to get a position here. Have been asked to stay and teach in the grades, and at the same time supervise the educational work of this church. I may accept, but hardly think so. There are several reasons, but the most outstanding is that the preacher here has fallen madly in love with me. Since I have finally tumbled, I realize why the invitations came so fast and urgently, and why he didn't take time to write but kept the wires hot. Well, I was as blind to it all as could be. This is going to make it a little embarrassing, but I am going to try my best to overcome it. He is one of the instructors and is a fine fellow, but I do not care for him in the least and never shall.

Now, if you want to do me a favor, write me real often and play the part of "my friend." See? All my mail comes to his box. If you don't have time to write, send some blank paper, but put your name on the envelope and mark your letters "personal." He may lose heart if he sees letters coming constantly. I hardly know what to do with him, for I don't know him very well, and the community is strange to me! He comes after me three times a day for meals, and insists on taking me someplace every night. Pretends that it is all in the interest of the church. I do need to be with him lots because of our relation to the school. Don't feel like flatly refusing him, when he seems to be trying to get me acquainted with the community. He is responsible for the school board offering me the position for this winter. Oh, what a mess, and still I am supposed not to know a thing about his trap. Of course, he hasn't mentioned that he cares for me, but it's more plainly stated in his actions than if he told me.

Haven't time to answer your questions now. Do so later. So long. Here he comes.

Jo

Dear Jo,

You are surely leading a busy life. I'm sorry this embarrassing situation has arisen to mar your Vacation School. Maybe I'd better come and help in the school and give this preacher a little competition. I'd enjoy it — provided he didn't get all the breaks.

This is the first of the series of letters you'll receive in the next few weeks, so be prepared to be bored to tears, for I'm a poor correspondent and you may have to listen to a lot of humdrum stuff that will make his company seem very entertaining.

There is always the wastebasket, however. Isn't that a consoling thought? Anyway, I'll put my whole name on the return card so he won't think I'm a girlfriend. I'll not be legalistic, however, and keep count on you, and your offer of "blank paper" ought to hold good both ways.

Very best wishes,

Blakey

Dear Blakey,

I seem to have gotten the fever. This is the second letter today. I find it great sport, too. Now, if you think I am worrying for fear you'll get the habit of writing every day, you surely have another think coming. I am thoroughly enjoying every one of them. You didn't know how much it meant, to be assured that when school is over there will be awaiting me a letter from Blakey.

Yesterday, I received no letter. Maybe I left town before the mail was all up. So today after church Mr. Perry handed me two, saying, "What is the meaning of all these letters marked 'personal'?" I said, "Well, <u>he</u> has gotten into the habit of labeling them 'personal' because all of my mail which is not labeled so when it reaches the St. Louis office, is opened." He just sort of stared at me, but said nothing. You need not label the others, for I'm sure he has seen enough so that he recognizes them. And about the duration of my acquaintance with Mr. Perry, I had never seen him until the last week in May, when I was teaching in the Harlan training school. That makes it more embarrassing, for I'm supposed to be blind to all his plans. Sometimes, I am amused at it all. At other times, I feel just as sorry for him as I can. Still at other times, it provokes me beyond measure. It is somewhat funny, for some of the people here call me "the preacher's woman." Doesn't that sound like mountaineers?

Good night, sweet dreams,

Jo

9

Dear Blakey,

Blakey, you're a peach! I've been looking forward to this letter for several days. However, when we came home from school at noon, there was no mail for me in the preacher's box. I thought you had gone back on me, for I had rather expected a letter yesterday. Then after dinner, as we were coming back toward my room, the postmaster came up and handed me your letter stating that since it was marked "personal," they could not put it in someone else's box without my consent. Ha! I gave permission, so there will be no difficulty henceforth.

I know you want to know how <u>we</u> are making it. Well, a little better since I am getting acquainted with other folk, but we are invited to the same place twice a day for meals, and I've been able to spend only <u>one</u> evening without him. Say, I wish you would come. I'm afraid, however, it wouldn't be safe, for I'm so hungry to see someone from home that I'm afraid I'd greet you like a long-lost relative, and of course that would never do.

Now about me answering every letter, I'll do my best. I ought to be willing to use the Golden Rule in the matter, hadn't I?

Heaps of thanks and good wishes,

> *Jo*

Dear Jo,

You don't know what temptation you put in my thoughts when you describe the greeting I might receive if I came, and as for its "never doing," it sounds delicious to me. I was glad your Friday Assembly was so successful, but didn't dream of anything else. You see, I have a high regard for your ability. And can't say I blame "the preacher" in the least for his ambitions. Now I'm not boosting for him. I'm just complimenting his judgment. Maybe I'd better go down to Kress's store and get a diamond ring to give him heart failure.

Good night and best wishes from your devoted friend,

> Blakey

Dear Jo,

Just returned from a nice long ride in the cool of the evening. I suppose I should have been home writing letters. I have several that need writing, including six brothers and sisters who might have cause to wonder if I were still alive if it were not the usual thing for me not to write.

Did I ever tell you of the "dirty trick" my oldest brother played on me with regard to my correspondence? Well, here goes:

Just before "the war" (doesn't that sound like an old-timer?), I went up into the northern part of Minnesota to work on a farm for the summer. As usual, I failed to write home when I got there, and in about two or three weeks I received a letter, typewritten, on a lawyer's stationery, saying that my brother, my roommate, my brother's girl, and the girl I'd been playing around with, were on their way to the golf links, and at a railroad crossing were all instantly killed.

I got that far and couldn't read any farther. I just laid the letter down and sat there for about twenty minutes — stunned. Then I thought I might as well read the rest, and the next paragraph said, "None of this has happened, but any of it might have happened and we wouldn't know how to get ahold of you." Well, it's a good thing I wasn't able to get ahold of <u>him</u> just then, or he might have wished it <u>had</u> happened. So, if I ever pull any practical jokes on you, you'll know where I got all my meanness.

Then, to think I'm writing you a letter every day. I don't do that for everybody, but it's been fun so far. It would be quite a joke indeed if I got the habit and couldn't stop. Wouldn't it?

Must close and get home to bed. Goodnight and pleasant dreams.

Impatiently,

Blakey

Dear Blakey,

Well, the preacher hasn't had much to say about your letters. I don't know whether they're having the desired effect or not, but I know he is aware of the fact that there is a Bernard B. Blakey who lives in Tulsa, Oklahoma. He hasn't slowed down his pace any, but maybe he will.

I wish you could take a drive through this beautiful country. I am anxious to contrast this with the Rockies. I am quite sure that there is no spot in the Rockies more beautiful. There are paved highways all through here, and the drives are simply wonderful.

Surely enjoy your letters. Don't worry about my becoming bored.

Do your letters go to your room or to the store? I imagine that the person who receives the mail must wonder who this newly found friend is. Ha!

All good wishes,

Jo

Dear Blakey,

Just two weeks more, and I shall be leaving. I rather dislike the idea of leaving, except that I do want to get away from Mr. Perry. What would you do if you were in my place? I can't go places by myself, for I do not know where people live. Have to be in a different home each day. Then, too, I am invited to homes all over this county (some of them are ten miles away.) Also, he is invited every place I am. I want to be nice to him on account of our relation to the work, and I ought to be able to do it for just this month. Yet, I do not want to give him any chance to believe that I am in the least interested in him. Goodness, what a mess!

I made a great big bow when I read what you said about my being able to add dignity to Vacation School management.

Be a good boy today,

> *Jo*

Dear Jo,

Back from Prayer Meeting, where our attendance fell to about twenty-six. I think I missed my calling. I should have been a preacher, only I can't deliver a sermon. I just preach to my friends. I'm handicapped in my preaching. I can't use the pulpit and have to do it with individuals and small groups. I need a home to which I could invite them.

Sincerely,

> Blakey

GRANDPA EVENTUALLY FOUND AN AUDIENCE FOR HIS SERMONS AND LECTURES AS DISCUSSION LEADER OF A GREAT BOOKS GROUP AT THE ANDREW CARNEGIE LIBRARY IN ENID, OKLAHOMA. MY MOM SAYS HE USED TO PRACTICE HIS DISCUSSION TECHNIQUES ON THE FAMILY, AT THE DINNER TABLE.

Dear Blakey,

I'm on the train again. We do not lack entertainment today. There is a bride and groom on this coach. How do I know? Why, it is evident in every move they make. They try to act absolutely natural and unassuming, and are really acting just the opposite. Then, their clothes look brand new and their handbags have never been used before. There are a number of things which give honeymooners away.

I have lots of fun observing people on the train and in train stations. I find it a good way to make use of long hours. Sometimes, I try to imagine who they are and where they're going and what they will do when they get there. Then I think it's great fun to try to detect from the facial expression, speech and actions, just what dispositions they have.

I'm thoroughly enjoying the good old Kansas plains. They're not as pretty as the mountains, but they look good to me because they are close to home.

See you tomorrow,

Jo

August 3, 1928 from Beulah, Colorado · Friday afternoon

Dear Blakey,

I wonder if you would like a cool breeze from the Rockies? If so, just read this letter a few times.

I'm sure you could not receive more enjoyment from my letters than I do from yours. The preacher tried to tell me that a daily letter was too often to write to anyone, and that they were bound to become monotonous. Well, he may know what he's talking about, but I know that I have received a great kick out of this adventure.

Night, night. Sweet dreams,

Jo

Dear Blakey,

I am sitting in front of my cabin just where you found me yesterday. I guess I should have been prepared for what happened last night but was not, and it was really quite a shock to me.

I surely was glad to have you, and enjoyed so much the short time which we spent together. I forgot to tell you that I enjoyed having dinner with you last night.

I don't know how soon I shall be able to give you an answer. Please give me plenty of time that I may think about it and pray about it. Blakey, are you sure that you really love me? It seems to me that we hardly know each other. Yet, I guess we do. Are you sure that I could fill Ione's place in your life?

I think no one would enjoy a lovely Christian home more than I. However, I think a home can be neither lovely nor Christian without love and devotion on the part of both husband and wife. There is no doubt in my mind about your being able to fulfill these essential requirements, and if I can come to the conclusion that I love you deeply enough, I shall be glad to enter into partnership with you.

Sincerest wishes,

Jo

JO WAS IN MISSOURI, PACKING TO GO TO ANOTHER ASSIGNMENT WHEN B.B. APPEARED, HAVING DRIVEN 300 MILES TO SEE HER. B.B. SAID, "I TOOK HER TO DINNER AND THEN WE DROVE OUT TO THE COUNTRY, WHERE I TOOK HER CHIN AND TURNED HER FACE UP, AND ASKED HER TO BE MY WIFE."

IT WAS THREE MONTHS BEFORE JO SAID YES TO B.B.'S PROPOSAL. SHE HESITATED, IN PART, BECAUSE SHE DIDN'T WANT TO SADDLE HIM WITH HER COLLEGE DEBT. BY THE TIME THEY WERE MARRIED, JO HAD ONE DOLLAR TO HER NAME, WHICH SHE GAVE TO HER HUSBAND. "I MARRIED HER FOR HER MONEY," B.B. WOULD JOKE.

1926

Dear JoJo,

Everyone asked where my wife was, as they always do when I've been gone twenty-four hours. My brother A.L. told everyone I'd gone "dear" hunting. Everyone has me married every time I turn around. So you see, you'll disappoint the entire East End of Tulsa if you don't accept.

I thought of you as I drove along and saw the sun painting the clouds, first a delicate rose, then deeper colors of lavender, purple, and even crimson. I wished we might take a long camping trip together as a honeymoon trip (not that I'm too sure of your answer, but I can wish at least), and camp by some lake or stream and watch the "Painter of Nature" color the skies just for you and me.

I'll dream of you,

Blakey

Dear Blakey,

Everyone who met you liked you immensely. Mrs. Furbish said to me, "Josephine, if I'm not badly mistaken, he's a real man." Then my girlfriend, Lucille Denny, said you made a very favorable impression on her. She could hardly wait to get to me after her class was over to inquire about you. You can rest assured that I had nothing but praise to say about you.

Maybe you think I didn't have to do some rushing today. Thought last night I had things pretty well ready to go, but this morning had to finish packing my books, teach two hours, grade all the notes for both my classes, make out my grade sheets, eat dinner, and get to my train by 1:15.

All good wishes,

Jo

Dearest JoJo,

Your two sweet letters came this morning and have caused me to want to get a pen in my hand every minute since their arrival. As to your two questions, I can truthfully answer "Yes" with all my heart.

I've dreamed of a home with a life partner to whom I could bring the joys and triumphs that may come to me, for they are so much sweeter if there is someone to share them; and when there are heartaches and discouragements, it surely helps to have a sympathetic ear to listen and encourage one. I've gloried in the accomplishments that you've achieved, and the times you've needed encouragement and sympathy and help have made me want to be near to help and shield and protect you.

These are all facts, but when I stop to analyze why I love you, it isn't just these things that can be put in words. It's just because you are you, which to me seems the best reason in the world. So many times when I've failed, I've realized that I could have succeeded with just a bit of help at just the right moment, and wonder if you've felt the same. Then, when I've succeeded, success has seemed so shallow because I had no one with whom to celebrate and share it.

Somehow, you just seem to fit into my dreams as though you belonged there. I've dreamed of a home where love made its continual abode, and its influence for good and right, in my dreams, seemed to spread far and wide, even across the seas.

I seem to be clear up in the clouds these days. My heart beats strong and true for you. And you may have all the time you need to find the answer, for I have complete faith that you'll do all that's right and good and fine and true. It's that knowledge that makes me love you and want you for my wife.

Lovingly,

Blakey

"IONE WAS A BEAUTIFUL WOMAN," B.B. ADMITTED, "BUT I GOT THE PRETTIEST ONE — IN A DIFFERENT WAY."

"SHE WAS THE BEAUTY QUEEN," JO RECALLS, "I WASN'T TOO GOOD-LOOKING, AND I KIND OF WORRIED ABOUT IT. BUT MY MOTHER PUT A SLOGAN IN MY HEAD THAT I STILL REMEMBER. 'BEAUTY IS AS BEAUTY DOES.'"

Dearest JoJo,

Brother Rhinehart has asked me to preach Sunday evening in his place. If I do, it will be my first sermon. It will require some deep thought and prayer. How I wish you were here to steady me and talk it over with me. This long-distance courtship places me at a disadvantage. Paper seems such a cold medium for expression and yet, how glad I am that I have even that.

I've many faults too. I've lived alone and left undone things that would have annoyed one living with me, contracted habits that will need to be changed. The work and planning of a home entices me and I ache to try to make it nice and comfortable and enticing for you. Not a showplace, nor an exclusive place, but one of taste and an inviting place (one that says, "Enter and rest and think").

I must get to bed, so I'll wish you a restful sleep and hope you waken thinking of,

Your Blakey

Dear Blakey,

In answer to your question as to which kind of a home I'd rather have, I can truthfully say I should like to have a real home. You know how I like my work. No one could be happier in any line of work than I am in mine, but I think it is only natural that any woman should dream of a home. I haven't had much time to think about it, for I've been too busy getting ready for a career and in being of service; but back in my subconscious mind, there has been that dream of a sweet Christian home.

I was so surprised the night you asked me to enter into partnership with you in making that home that I was not prepared to ask you the scores of questions which I want to ask before I can feel that I really know you. I realize now that you had a right to think that I would be prepared.

JoJo

Dearest JoJo,

I was reading some Italian Proverbs today, and one said, "He who is not impatient is not in love." See?

Good night and pleasant dreams,

Blakey

Dearest JoJo,

Be mighty careful about the person with whom you look at the moon. I'm going to enter an order for a full moon when I come to see you. I believe it would help lots. And at 10:15 tonight I'll be looking at it too, and wishing we might be looking at it together instead of so far apart.

I'd love to have you out in a canoe tonight, just floating along, and drinking in the moonlight and your presence. The very thought gives me a feeling of peace and calm and contentment.

Heaps o' love,

Blakey

Sweetheart JoJo,

I love you, love you. I just seem to want to tell you that over and over again. I hope it will never grow old to your ears, that it will always seem sweet to hear me say it, that it will bring memories and anticipation to your mind and an answering thrill to your heart.

I want to help and encourage and protect you, to inspire and expand your ideals and services to the world.

I need your help and encouragement and cooperation to make the most of my life. I need you desperately. I want you to need me and depend upon me even as I do upon you. I want our lives to be so completely one life that we can have our joys and sorrows, our triumphs and defeats, in one common store.

I want that we should put our shoulders together in joint tasks to labor and grow together, that our ideals and purposes and goals shall be one, and that those ideals and purposes and goals may be Christian, that each of us may lend the other a helping hand to steady each other as we go, making allowance for the shortcomings of each of us but helping to overcome these.

Sweetheart, I can't find the words to tell you how much I care. My arms ache to go around your shoulders and hold you close to me and feel that we are one being, to sense the fragrance of your presence, to know that you are finding pleasure in my nearness and my love for you, to know that someone needs and depends upon me not to fail them.

Dearest, there is no worse feeling than to believe you are just not needed. I wish you could know how your letter warmed my heart when you said you wished and wished for me when you were having such a terrible time in Chicago.

Now, lest I just bubble off completely, I'm just going to say I love you, love you, love you, and sign your,

Blakey

Dear Blakey,

So you would like to know more about my family? Well, it would take much more time and paper than I have at my disposal to tell you as much as I could about all of them. There are so many of us that I expect I'd better tell you most of it when I see you. There are eleven children, and we're all living, only four married. You asked if there were any girls. Yes, there are five of us. Two of those are married. Relative to the looks of my single sisters, I'll let you be the judge. One is a brunette and the other is a blonde. They were here the day you came, but there were so many extras here that day that I am sure you didn't get them separated in such a short time. My single sisters are younger than I. One is twenty-three and the other nineteen. I'll try to find some Kodak pictures to send you soon. I do not think I answered you about exchanging pictures. I have not had a good picture taken since I was in college. However, I'd be tickled pink to have one of yours.

I was straightening up some of my things this morning and counted the letters which I've received from you. Can you guess how many? Have received seventy-five. I suppose you have received about that many from me. If so, those are more letters than I've written to all other boyfriends put together. I've never written oftener than once a week to any other man. Strange, isn't it? Can you guess the reason? Somehow, I can't feel sorry that it's happening this way. I've asked God to show me how to care for you, if that be His will, and I think He is answering me, for sometimes I get mighty lonesome for you, Blakey. If I could always feel as I feel now, I could go anyplace with you. I shall not be satisfied, however, until I talk with you again, for there are so many things involved.

Must be going, Bye Bye,

Jo

Dearest Jo,

What do folks call me? Well, that depends. Lois Mae calls me Uncle Bernard. A.L. calls me B.B. His wife Frances calls me Bernard. Folks at the church usually call me Brother Blakey. Mrs. Fred Winters calls me Bee. Mrs. Porter calls me Blakey and I suspect that some folks, when I'm not around, call me that Blankety Blank Blank that thinks he knows it all, so just take your choice. My old Auntie calls me Bernie Boy and Roy's wife, whom we've nicknamed Peg, calls me Peg's Bad Boy, and Roy calls me the Bad Blakey Boy. Some more to choose from!

It is some rush to get a few thousand dollars' worth of Christmas goods on their way to us and our Fall goods displayed, pottery unloaded and stored away, and run a Sunday school and do the publicity for a revival service, attend a city-wide training school, one-day conventions, and win a wife three hundred miles away. All at the same time. So please be patient with me. And

Love,

Blakey

WHEN GRANDMA AND GRANDPA WERE
IN THEIR NINETIES AND WOULD VISIT
MY UNCLE IN HIS NEW YORK LOFT, THEY
HAD TO SLEEP ON SEPARATE COUCHES.
IN THE MORNING, GRANDMA WOULD
CRAWL IN WITH GRANDPA TO CUDDLE.
"WHAT IS WITH YOU TWO? CAN'T YOU
SLEEP APART FOR EVEN ONE NIGHT?" MY
UNCLE WOULD ASK, TEASINGLY. "SOME-
ONE NEEDS TO THROW SOME COLD
WATER ON THESE TWO."

Dear Blakey,

We are all very glad that you came. It really seems like a dream to me. I hope you didn't have any trouble getting home. Did you get home by 1 o'clock? I'll bet you're some tired and sleepy man today, but maybe you can have a good rest tonight.

My Cousin Adeline remarked that she was glad that you seem to like children, and that her children didn't seem to worry you. They are so used to romping with their Daddy that they think they ought to play with others who come to the house. I guess you halfway realize how crazy I am about them.

I enjoyed especially our little visits. Really enjoyed them more than I did just talking about ourselves. It really shocks me when I think how I let you fondle me. I realize that it is my fault, and I'm not blaming you in the least. I think the reason I allowed those liberties is that I felt that you were hungry to see me; also, I realized that perhaps it will be some time before we see each other again. But, Blakey, I want you to know that I am not in the habit of allowing men the liberties which I allowed you. Never before have I allowed any gentleman friend to kiss me. I allowed you to do so only because we don't get to be together often. Really, I want to learn to love you, and feel that the process ought to be gradual. I wish we might have many opportunities just to visit with each other.

I enjoyed yesterday afternoon's visit immensely. I am sure that you are interested in the same things that I am, and that if I can learn to love you as you do me, we can unite our lives in a beautiful way. Please tell me what you think of what I've said. The next time we meet, let's have some good visits and learn to know each other. Now, I don't want that you not show me any affections, but I do not want to feel that I have to be on my guard all the time.

Your complaining,

JoJo

Dearest Jo,

Dearest, I suppose I should feel repentant for the liberties I took, but for the life of me I can't when I think of the thrill that went through me as I felt your arms about my neck and your lips against mine as we stood there in the moonlight. Please give me credit for considerable willpower though, in that I didn't try it again just as we were parting, for I wanted to do so in the most compelling way, and refrained only because I sensed your desire that I shouldn't.

Your unrepentant lover,

Blakey

Dear Blakey,

So Mrs. Winters asked you about your wife? Well, maybe someday, you won't have to answer in the negative. I know you think I'm as fickle about this as can be, but it's rather hard to make up my mind about the matter. If I could have, I surely would have told you just how I feel. Sometimes I feel one way, and sometimes another, but Adeline and Clifford tell me that it is natural, since I have been thinking for some time in terms of a career; also since we don't get to see each other often, it is hard really to know each other.

Heaps of good wishes to my Blakey,

JoJo

Dearest Jo,

Honey, I get mighty lonesome for you. You fill a great big place in my life. I hope you just keep on "slipping" until you are engulfed in love for me and I in my love for you. I know happiness doesn't consist in what one has, but in what one is, yet the having doesn't hinder if it's connected with the being. I'm working to give you all I can, see?

Heaps o' love from,

Your hopeful Blakey

Dear Blakey,

Last night, after I wrote your letter, I decided to sit up and wait for the Shirleys to return before retiring. They didn't come home until eleven. It was the first time I have been afraid in a long, long time, but for some reason I couldn't feel comfortable.

I know you will feel good when I tell you that I wished and wished for you. It just seemed as if a part of me was missing (the courageous and protecting part of me). Does this sound like I love you? I know it does, but honey, I don't care. Do you? I am beginning to realize more and more how much you mean to me, and I don't believe I could be happy without you now. I think we might as well begin to plan for the future, so when I come down, we shall do so. When would you like to be married? I'm afraid I couldn't possibly do so before next summer.

I've been over an hour writing this, for I could hardly make myself tell you these things. Now I feel much better. It's been hard to write you lately, for I've been fighting to keep from telling you for fear I might change my mind. I'm sure, though, that I do love you, and I'm also sure that I shall love you more as I know you better.

Must be going. With love,

JoJo

GRANDPA LATER DESCRIBED WHAT PROMPTED GRANDMA TO ACCEPT HIS PROPOSAL: "JO WAS IN ENID, TAKING CARE OF THE SHIRLEY CHILDREN AND WRITING A LETTER TO ME, WHEN A LITTLE MOUSE GOT TO CHEWING ON SOME PAPER SOMEWHERE, AND THE NOISE KIND OF SCARED HER. THE VERY NEXT DAY SHE ACCEPTED MY PROPOSAL, SO I OWE MY HAPPINESS TO A MOUSE."

Dearest JoJo,

Read this before my picture, just as though I were speaking to you. Please.

I haven't one bit of news this evening. I can't even think of one tiny scrap of news to tell you just now, but I want to chat with you awhile.

I wish you were near so that I might draw your arm about my shoulder and snuggle up close. Someway, I feel just like a tired little boy who needs to be petted and loved a little bit. Would you do that for me if you were here, dear? I imagine you stroking my hair just in a possessive way, and dear, I do so want to just belong to you, and for you to just belong to me. Someway, that would just give me more strength and courage than anything I know, and I feel I need that now.

I just know that both of us would be in an understanding mood and that our thoughts would travel along together without the need of words to express them. That our determination each to help the other would grow within us as we sat there together. That each of us would resolve to forget self in the advancement of our partnership in life. That faithfulness, trust, and loyalty and love would fill both of us.

I wonder if the desire for the fulfillment of this little "dream" of mine fills your heart too. Somehow, I'm sure it does. Is that egotistical? I don't mean it that way, but I know you love me a little, at least. God grant that it may grow and grow until both our lives are filled with love, one for another.

Sweetheart, I just want to say, I love you, in a million different ways and languages tonight. It is an overpowering desire. How I hope you'll understand and that it will meet an answering desire in your heart as you read this, and that it won't sound silly.

I love you, JoJo. I do truly,

Your Blakey

Dear Blakey,

The proofs to my pictures were terrible. I wanted a picture which looks straight at folk, and the photographer didn't let me do so. I kept them two days; then went back and asked to have two additional sittings. He gladly consented. I truly hope they are good. If they are not, I shall feel quite provoked. I really think he's a poor photographer. It may be, however, that the proofs look too much like me. Ha!

I wish you were here to keep me company. I'm lonesome for you tonight. Why <u>can't</u> we be closer together? I'd better change the topic of conversation lest I tell you that I love you. I know that I have never felt toward any man as I feel toward you, and it may be love in its infancy.

You may be sure that the things which you said sounded all but silly. Really, I should miss them dreadfully if you failed to say them. I trust that you will never cease to tell me how much you love me. If I thought you would, I don't believe I could consent to marry you. I feel sure, however, that as our love for each other grows, those things will take care of themselves.

Night, night. Sweet dreams from,

Your uncertain Jo

Dearest Sweetheart,

I wonder if you have any realization of the mixture of feelings that are running through my nerves, dear. Joy, that I'm to have you for a life partner. Determination with a capital D, to strive to make you happy and comfortable; of responsibility and desire to make good, but most of all, dear, of just blind love for you. I'm just aching all over to have my arms about you and to whisper my love in your ear, and I just feel sure "the guard" would not be up, but there would be sweet surrender and an answering light in your eyes and manner.

How I wish I had an aeroplane. I'd come right over right now, and just carry you away.

Dear, there is a prayer in my heart, too, that God will bless our lives together, making them useful and fruitful of good.

Oceans of love from,

Your own Blakey

My Own JoJo,

I've read your two letters so often that I could almost repeat them from memory. I've gotten almost nothing accomplished today, because my mind seems to have been in Enid with you, or in the future with us. "Do I care" if it sounds like you love me? Dearest, I've been waiting to hear that for ages. I've dreamed about it, prayed about it, thought about it, longed for it, and now it has come about. And sweetheart, I love you too with my whole heart.

As Brother Goff was preaching tonight, I couldn't help visualizing myself waiting at the altar and your own radiant self coming slowly down the aisle toward me and a feeling of thanksgiving and peace came into my heart.

When would I like to be married, dear? I'd like to be married to you tomorrow. I don't want to waste one day more without you unnecessarily.

Your own lover,

Blakey

Dear Blakey,

Dr. Smith began to tease me about remaining single. Said he thought perhaps if I had that "come hither" look in my eye, I wouldn't be having such a time. As he shook my hand, he told me to lasso "him." Then I led him to your picture on the piano and said to meet "him." Both the Smiths and the Harrisons looked <u>amazed</u>. They all said you were mighty good-looking. The only thing they regret is that you're not a preacher, for they think I ought to be the helpmate of some good preacher. Well, I guess a number of others will be shocked when they realize that I'm not to be an old maid. But I don't care. It'll be good for them.

> *Night night, honey,*
>
> *Jo*

Sweetheart O' Mine,

You can't imagine how I missed you last night. I think my visit with you and your folk has helped me greatly, for I realize now that I love you much more than I did before. Honey, <u>I do love you</u>. I wanted to tell you when I was with you, but I guess I was too timid. I've never been in love before, and it embarrasses me somewhat.

I am as eager as I can be to start our little home. I am willing that we build gradually, and that we start with only what you can afford, but of course I would like to have things as nice as can be afforded. I don't want to <u>try</u> to live above our means, so just rest assured that Jo will stand by you in whatever is best. Of course, I have no idea what you have been able to save, but that doesn't concern me. I would give lots if I had been able to save something which I could use.

> *Gobs of love just for my Big Boy,*
>
> *Jo*

Dear Bernard,

Have you discovered what your folks think of me? I enjoyed every minute of my visit with them, and, honey, I wouldn't take heaps for <u>our</u> visits. You mean much more to me than you did before I came down. I'm eager to help you found the home you have wanted for so many years.

Honey, I love you,

JoJo

Darling Jo,

My whole family seems to think I'm a good picker. Honey, next summer seems such a long time to wait. I'll get to see you only occasionally. I know, dear, that you'll set the date as soon as you can and I'm not complaining.

Your own sweetheart,

Bernard

Dearest Sweetheart,

Honey, would it make much difference as to whether I call you Bernard or B.B.? I like B.B. better, but if it makes any difference, I shall school myself to say the other.

Saturday night, I could have talked with you for hours. Just think, it won't be long until I won't have to send you home, but instead, I'll just welcome you home in the evenings. Sometimes I get so thrilled that I wonder if I can wait until June. It really is shocking how I think constantly in terms of our home. If someone had suggested a few months ago that I would be so enthusiastic about my marriage, I would have laughed at the idea.

Bushels of love just for you,

Your own JoJo

Darling Jo,

Tonight is a rainy, stormy night that makes one long for a big armchair, a good cozy fire, a good book in his hand, and a sweet wife sitting on his lap, her head on his shoulder and her arm about his neck, and they discuss the book and relate experiences recalled to memory by the book.

It is a nice man who can enjoy to the full, both the getting and the having and then the giving. I don't know how to work out a schedule in these busy times for family worship to be included, but I want us to have a time set apart to worship together daily. In drawing us closer to Christ it will draw us closer to each other, just as everything which is drawn toward the center of a circle draws nearer to everything else so drawn. I do not want us to grow lopsided, intellectually or spiritually.

I've preached long enough, so I'll quit and just whisper a little news in your ear — "I love you." (You didn't know that did you? What! You did?) I must go to bed before I go to sleep and you learn all my deep dark secrets.

Dreamily yours,

Blakey

My Lover,

I'm deeply interested in what you say about family worship. Of course we shall have it. I know the American family life is not as it once was, and that it is hard to find a regular time for such things; but honey, I want our home to have that atmosphere of restfulness and peace which so many homes lack. Let's make Christ the head of our home, and give Him full sway. What do you say?

Must be going to bed. Sweet dreams from the girl who loves you the most,

JoJo

GRANDPA NEVER GAVE UP HIS LOVE OF LEARNING. EVEN AFTER HE LOST MOST OF HIS EYESIGHT, HE CONTINUED TO READ LARGE-PRINT BOOKS USING A MAGNIFYING GLASS THAT HE WORE CONSTANTLY ON A STRING AROUND HIS NECK. WHEN HE WAS NINETY-TWO, HE SIGNED UP FOR A CLASS IN ESTATE PLANNING AT THE MINNEAPOLIS COMMUNITY COLLEGE.

Dearest Sweetheart,

Honey, there's a favor which I'm going to ask you to do for yourself. I wanted to ask you yesterday, but was afraid you would misconstrue my motives. But sweetheart, you've been so busy taking care of your business for the church and for me that you have forgotten your personal appearance. If I didn't love you a lot, I wouldn't tell you this, but I know you'll understand. It makes me just want to hasten our wedding day so that I can be the encouragement you have not had. You are just too fine a man to neglect yourself. You are so interested in big things that you haven't given as much time to these little things as you should, for instance keeping your suits pressed, your shoes shined, and wearing ragged cuffs on Sunday. I think it very natural that you should be a bit careless, but honey, JoJo wants you to look just as nice as you are.

Bushels of love from your complaining,

> *Jo*

My Darling JoJo,

Your smiling face is looking at me from the dresser by my side. Someway tonight, it has a sort of an expectant look, as though it just knew I must measure up to the best that is in me. Someway it's growing on me so that I can see the real you in it. I wouldn't part with it for worlds.

Heaps o' love to my sweetheart from your,

> Blakey

GRANDMA HAS SAID THAT IN THE
HISTORY OF THEIR MARRIAGE THERE
WAS NEVER A DAY THAT GRANDPA
DIDN'T TELL HER THAT HE LOVED HER.
GRANDPA WOULD SAY "THERE WAS A
MAN WHO TOLD HIS WIFE, 'IF EVER I
DON'T LOVE YOU, I'LL TELL YOU.' BUT
THAT IS NOT US, I THINK WE SHOULD BE
USING THOSE THREE WORDS EVERY DAY.
I LOVE YOU."

Sweetheart O' Mine,

I didn't like your picture when I first saw it, but honey, I've changed my mind. I think it's good because, as I look at it again and again, each time suggests by the expression something new and fine about you that I hadn't put into definite thought before. It seems to be continually changing, just as you keep showing me different sides of your nature, each more lovely than the last. When I woke this morning, the first thing I did was to move a chair so I might say good morning to my sweetheart.

When just your picture gives me so much joy, I can hardly contain myself in waiting for the reality. Even my active imagination cannot picture the joy I'm anticipating.

I tell you of my love so often that I fear you will find it becoming monotonous and think I'm trying to fill space in my letters, but this is far from the truth. I just tingle with the desire to make you happy.

Love and kisses from your dreaming lover,

Blakey

November 21, 1928 from Tulsa, Oklahoma

Sweetheart O' Mine,

I decided that the failure of many marriages was simply lack of the determination to agree. I've always said that if I ever did get married, it would be for life. There was to be no turning and looking back. So I've put every thought that doesn't lead to our united lives so far from me that it seems as though we ought to be married now. The trouble with many marriages, I believe, is that one or both keep wondering what life would have been if they had made a different choice.

Honey, someway I just know we are going to be as happy as larks together.

Goodnight, dear heart, and sweet dreams,

Your own loving Blakey

Once, when I asked Grandpa about his secret to longevity, he replied, "Eat all the salt and sugar you want, refuse all vegetables, and have an ancestor who lived to be 109." When he reached his nineties, Grandpa had only two teeth, and he used to say "Thank god they meet." He ate Campbell's soup almost every day.

My Darling JoJo,

When I asked my sister-in-law Frances how much her grocery bill was, she figured for the three of them it averaged $43.65 per month. So, for two, we ought to get by for $30, which is only about three or four dollars more than I spend for food myself.

I think my tastes in food are not expensive at all. I like meats but can get along without them. I'm really fond of rice cooked in a good many different ways. I suppose I do not use a pound of butter a year, unless on toast, and I could eat soup about three times a day, and like things done over in some other form than that in which they originally appeared. In fact I really think I won't be hard to cook for.

Perhaps my greatest fault is my easygoing disposition, and I'll need a few jolts such as you gave me about my personal appearance.

It is after midnight so I must get to bed, dear. I've enjoyed this little chat with my sweetheart.

Heaps o' love and kisses from your lover,

B.B.B.

GRANDMA AND GRANDPA GAVE THEIR CHILDREN THE MOST IMPORTANT GIFTS — ROOTS AND WINGS.

WHEN ROY WAS FIFTEEN YEARS OLD AND MARIAN WAS TWELVE, GRANDPA AND GRANDMA LET THEM TAKE THE TRAIN OVERNIGHT TO TEXAS TO SEE AN ICE SKATING SHOW. LATER, WHEN ROY TOLD THEM THAT HE WANTED TO BE AN ICE SKATER, THEY TRUSTED HIM TO MAKE THE RIGHT DECISION FOR HIS LIFE. HIS DECISION TO BECOME A PROFESSIONAL ICE SKATER TOOK HIM TWICE AROUND THE WORLD.

Sweetheart O' Mine,

I worked at the store until 8:30, then came home and lighted a fire and enjoyed an hour with the *National Geographic* in an airplane ride from Constantinople to Athens, above the battlefields of the Greeks and Trojans, above the fording place of the Turks, of Alexander and the Persians, above the scene of the naval engagement where the Allies attempted to free the Dardanelles in 1915, above the scenes of the travels of the Apostles Paul, Silas, Timothy, Barnabas and Luke.

How I wish some lecturer with ready tongue and movie camera could catch the spirit of adventure in mythology, in Holy Scripture, in modern geography, and take it to every high school freshman and inspire them with the desire to know and understand the background, the life, ideals and fine things of other lands, and to build up a worldwide spirit of brotherhood.

Sweetheart, I love you with all my heart. Your lover,

Bernard

My Sweetheart,

So, Mr. Mayfield asked you to preach? I'm really proud of my lover to think that, even though he is not a preacher, he is privileged to speak to church audiences. But just you wait, when the lady preacher comes on the scene, we will show them who's who, won't we? Ha! Now, don't you worry, for I'll not advertise the fact that I'm supposed to be a preacher.

Must be going. See you tomorrow. Heaps of love,

Jo

Sweetheart O' Mine,

Your picture is surely a comfort to me, dear, but it just can't reach out and put its arm about me, nor speak to me in words, and I want the real you so badly.

I've been scheming and planning to know just what is the best thing for us to do in regard to our home. I really think that perhaps it would be well for us to sell the car if we can get what it is worth, or trade it in on the house.

I've got something to work for now, when before everything seemed dark and I didn't care whether I amounted to anything or not. That seems awful to confess, but I might as well tell the truth and be square about it.

Your devoted lover,

B.B.B.

My Very Own Sweetheart,

My stationery and I have quite a time making connections. Oh well, the time will come when I won't try to have three or four homes, but will have all my belongings in one home — our home. I wish there weren't so many months between this and the month when that will be true.

Adeline and I have been doing some planning. I would very much like to have a church wedding, and we have decided it will not cost much more than a home wedding. I read the letter you wrote to Adeline. It was sweet of you to say what you did about plans for our wedding. Now, don't you worry about being <u>just</u> a necessary detail. Folk will be looking you over from head to foot, since you're from another community. Ha!

If you should walk into this room right now, I'd just about squeeze you to pieces. I do love you with all my heart. You know I do, don't you, even though I can't always tell you so with my lips. I mean verbally, for I do tell you every time my lips touch yours.

Heaps and heaps of love from your very own,

> *Jo*

Dearest B.B.,

My hope chest is beginning to grow already. My family is all interested. They're beginning to make tea towels, embroider hand towels, etc. Last night my sister Maude brought me a beautiful changeable-colored silk pillow. It's quite a delight to plan and work on things for our home. It's especially nice that Mother and my sisters are interested, for it will be a little hard for me to do much while constantly on the go.

Heaps of love,

> *Jo*

My First Love,

And now I must get back into the habit of writing a letter each day to my Big Boy; it's lots of fun. I've been quite sleepy all day. Have been keeping late hours with "a gentleman from another city." You are simply indispensable to me now. It would be mighty hard to give you up.

I trust you had a pleasant trip home. Somehow, your visit this time meant more to me than all the others put together. Maybe it was because I was able to do one or two things for you. Maybe it was because I know you better. It seems the more I know you, the more I love you.

Honey, write to your JoJo and tell her you love her. Good night. Sweetest of dreams,

   JoJo

My Own JoJo,

   How I enjoyed our little parties in the kitchen, watching you sew on my buttons and dreaming of when we will assume our privileges as partners each of the other. Won't it be great when we can do things for the other and our partnership? Better come tuck in your big boy for the night.

   Your sleepyheaded lover,

      B.B.

My Own Lover,

Last night, I wanted you as badly as I've ever wanted anything in all my life. As I sat by the fire with your picture in my hand, how I wished that instead of only a likeness of you, it was the real you into whose eyes I could look. Honey, how much do you love your JoJo? She loves you much more than she is able to tell.

Night Night,

   Jo

GRANDMA AND GRANDPA WERE MARRIED
ON JULY 14, 1929. ON OCTOBER 29, 1929,
THE STOCK MARKET CRASHED, LEADING
THE COUNTRY INTO A LONG DEPRESSION.

THEIR HOPES AND DREAMS CHANGED
DRAMATICALLY, AS GRANDPA AND HIS
BROTHER LOST THEIR HARDWARE STORE.
THEY MOVED TO ENID, OKLAHOMA,
WHERE GRANDPA GOT A JOB IN THE BUSI-
NESS OFFICE AT PHILLIPS UNIVERSITY,
WHICH WAS GRANDMA'S ALMA MATER.

January 1, 1929 from Tulsa, Oklahoma

Dearest JoJo,

Happy New Year! May the new year bring you all that is good and fine and true, and naught that is ill or false, and may each succeeding year be better than the last. This is my New Year's wish for the sweetest girl in all the world, my Jo. Honey, you grow more dear to me each day. So much a part of me that to give up hope of you would be like tearing my very life in two. I hope and believe we shall grow together to be just one. Working, planning, serving, dreaming as one. Sweetheart, I love you with my whole heart and shall, not only through 1929, but through all my life and beyond

The new year is just upon the threshold. I wonder just what it holds in store for us, you and I? Happiness, prosperity, labor, and service with each other and for each other, growth together, and play and recreation. All of these, I hope, perhaps seasoned with a few trials and crosses to develop us. But with courage we can surmount them all, I'm sure.

Bushels of love to you, dear, from your lover,

B.B.B.

January 9, 1929 from Tulsa, Oklahoma · Wednesday evening

My Sweetheart,

I am interested in your work, dear, in the friends you make, the problems you meet. Won't you write to me just like you do in your diary? Tell me all your hopes and joys and disappointments, too, for I want to share your joy and try to make up for some of the sorrows.

Who was it said, "Sharing our joys doubles them and sharing our sorrows cuts them in half"? I've tried it with you and I know it's true. Hold your breath, shut your eyes and imagine a great hug and kiss from your lover,

B.B.B.

50

My Dearest B.B.,

Why haven't I heard from you since Monday? Sometimes I miss a day but I've missed two whole days. I even called at the window today to be sure. Maybe you've written and my letters are being held up here.

You said for me to write to you just like I write my diary, registering my exact feelings. I'm afraid I can't do that just now. You would be shocked, for I'm as lonesome and blue as can be. What has happened, honey? Why haven't you written? It takes something like this to make me realize how much you mean to me, I guess.

Your lonesome girl,

Jo

Sweetheart O' Mine,

Honey, I don't want to make a fuss about <u>verbal expressions</u> of appreciation for meals, but when I read what you said about <u>the amount</u> you eat being a first-class testimony, I couldn't help but think of the scores of homes I know where men do "just eat ravenous amounts" but say nothing. Oh well, let's wait until we get to that bridge before we cross it, what do you say? Now, don't get all excited and imagine me nagging about it. I won't do that. In the first place, there'll be no need to do so. In the second place, even if occasions warranted it, I think nagging is unpardonable.

Yes, I am lonesome for my lover. Sometimes I get so lonesome, I just feel as if I must cry. That night when I went home so terribly lonesome and blue, your picture was a great consolation. Honey, it would be unbearable to have to give you up now. I can begin to realize how terrible it must be to lose one you love.

Must be going to lunch. See you tomorrow. Bushels of love,

Jo

"Could hardly wait to get to the post office to get B.B.'s letters, but there was no mail for me. At noon I made a special trip back to the post, but the empty box stared me in the face again.

"This agony is terrible, I can't imagine why he doesn't write. I've been sitting here for forty-five minutes with his picture in my hand wondering if he is tired of me, or if he has gone back to Ione. I wish I could shake this terrible spell."

… from Jo's diary, January 16, 1929

My Own Darling,

Do you realize that just exactly one year ago tonight you wrote me your first letter? Tonight I sorted out all your letters and arranged them chronologically. I've lost the envelopes from two of them. I wanted to reread them so often that I did not put all of them back in the envelopes. Now don't you feel complimented? I wonder if you read my letters as often as I do yours? Perhaps you are too timid to say.

It has seemed ages since October 15, when you first wrote me that you loved me, only a little more than three months, and still longer ages until June when we shall belong to each other. What a joy you have been to me! How I would have gotten along without your daily letters I surely do not know. I surely must write to Kentucky and thank that preacher. Ha!

Have you been there long enough to get acquainted? May I come down to see you soon? I'm oh so hungry to see you. I've spent so much time with your letters that it is almost midnight and I must get to bed, honey.

Come put your arms about my neck and give a great big kiss to,

Your Big Boy

My Own Lovely Lady,

Sweetheart, you have told me very little about your home life, the folk with whom you work, what hours you keep. Please do not think I'm complaining. I am not in that sort of mood in the least. I enjoy every word of your letters, but I'm interested in the little homely things of your life. Whether or not the rooms are kept warm, how much of the time you are left to yourself, whether there is a chance for recreation and relaxation, whom you have found to be congenial friends. A thousand and one questions.

Your own B.B.

Sweetheart O' Mine,

So you think I've been keeping too quiet about everyday affairs? Forgive me, honey. I surely didn't mean not to keep you properly informed. The fact of the matter is that absolutely nothing exciting happens while I'm at home. I live with Mrs. Hicks who teaches the older women's Bible class. She's a splendid woman, though terribly "set" in her ways. I make myself absolutely at home.

There's only one thing I do not like about my stay, and that is her little bulldog, Bobby, which she treats as if he were a child, and Bobby insists upon loving me, and I don't enjoy his demonstrations. I never have cared to have a dog or cat wallow all over me. I'm trying my very hardest to make myself like Bobby. I dislike appearing to be too nicey nice. Does my Big Boy like dogs? If so, I'll try not to be rude about those things.

When I go home in the evenings I usually visit with Mrs. Hicks and listen to the radio until about 8. Then go to my room and read or do my mending, or visit a little with my lover — through his picture. I am usually in bed by 9:30 or 10:00. As soon as I get my paycheck this month, I want to purchase some pieces of handwork to work on for my hope chest.

In the mornings, I arise at 7:30. Try to leave the house by five or ten minutes after 8:00. Stop downtown for breakfast. Go to the post office to get my mail. Usually arrive at the church about 8:45.

Sweetheart, my love matches yours, I think. Probably it hasn't been as long-standing, but it is firm and true.

Jo

B.B., My Lover,

Now, put on your shock absorbers. The Kentucky Bible School Association has chosen me to do their elementary work. Honey, you may be sorry to have me so far away, but I'm just as thrilled as can be. I'll be making $35 per week and will have all expenses paid. Then too, you know how I love the Kentucky people. I am right happy to spend this time with them. It will be my last opportunity.

Heaps of love,

Jo

Lovely Lady Love,

You'd better get an armor before I come, for fear I'll hold you so tight I'll break a rib. I'm just that hungry for you. Honey, I'm sending a whole trainload of love to my Valentine from,

Your B.B.

Pal O' Mine,

Honey, you make me love you almost to the point of desperation when your heart is all aflutter, as you say. How I've dreamed of this trip with you as my bride. No cares nor worries, driving when we please, stopping when we please, staying as long as we please. Having to be nowhere. Camping in the mountains or near a stream or lake. Buying our groceries from the farmers, cooking them over our gasoline stove and sitting by a campfire listening to my sweetheart tell me stories in the evening.

Your Big Boy

"... AND NO LETTER WHEN I WENT TO THE POST OFFICE. HOWEVER, MR. HUNTER CAME A LITTLE LATER AND HANDED ME ONE. AND WHAT A SWEET ONE IT WAS! B.B. HAD RECEIVED THREE OR FOUR LETTERS AND MY PHOTO. I HOPE HE LEARNS TO LOVE THAT PICTURE.

"MY HOW I WISH I COULD HAVE SOME MONEY ONCE IN A WHILE SO THAT I COULD WORK ON MY HOPE CHEST. MY HANDS ARE SIMPLY TIED; I GO WINDOW SHOPPING EVERY DAY AND JUST LOOK AND DREAM. YET I NEED CLOTHES SO BADLY THAT I WOULDN'T FEEL LIKE GETTING THINGS FOR MY HOPE CHEST EVEN IF I HAD SOME MONEY."

... FROM JO'S DIARY, FEBRUARY 22, 1929

GRANDMA AND GRANDPA RETIRED IN 1962, BOUGHT A HOUSE TRAILER, AND SPENT SOME TEN YEARS ON THE ROAD, RESEARCHING THEIR FAMILY HISTORIES. AFTER MOVING TO MINNESOTA, THEY SPENT ANOTHER TEN YEARS COMPILING THREE BOOKS.

GRANDMA WROTE BOOKS FOR BOTH SIDES OF HER FAMILY, *An Osburn Family 1750–1970* AND *A Walker Family 1800–1976*. GRANDPA'S RESEARCH FOR *A Blakey Book 1686–1977* TOOK LONGER AND COVERED A MUCH LONGER TIME PERIOD.

My Own Lover,

I am hardly over the shock about your having to leave so suddenly. And I was planning so much on our little visit all alone by the fireside tonight. If you were here, I'd let you love me a little and wouldn't push you away. I know how many times you did want to love me and I'm sorry, honey.

Honey, I'm mighty sorry about this grief through which you are going. I'm sorry I didn't have the privilege of knowing your grandmother. You've been fortunate to have a grandmother all these years, and I've never known one. Wish I could be with you to comfort you. I'm sure it will help just to know that I share your grief. She's my grandmother, too.

Must be going. I trust the oceans of love and the flood of kisses I am sending will not get lost before it reaches my first and only love.

JoJo

My Own Sweetheart,

Grandmother was almost ninety years old, and I am sure she felt ready to go. Grandfather and five of her children were already "over there."

Tonight I've been preparing a diagram of my family tree. Not that I think one amounts to any more simply because his ancestors amounted to something, but their worth often encourages one to be more useful himself. Since Father and Mother died when I was young, I've been interested in knowing as much about them as I can find out, and about aunts, uncles, and cousins, etc. I plan to get this information in just as good form as I can and make a scrapbook of it and illustrate it with pictures like those in my album, with a write-up about each one. I should like to make it in a form that will be prized as an heirloom after I'm gone from this world.

Your aging lover,

B.B.

My Own Sweetheart,

I'm getting so thrilled about the prospect of going to Seattle that I am living clear up in the clouds. Wouldn't it be lovely to have all your family at our wedding? Sure, we'll give them each an urgent invitation. Now I'm sure ours will be a church wedding. Adeline's house couldn't hold our families very well.

Must do some telephoning, so shall seal up a mountain of love in this letter and send it speeding to my sweetheart.

Jo

AT A TIME WHEN GRANDMA WAS PAYING FOR GROCERIES ON CREDIT, GRANDPA OFTEN TOOK MONEY FROM HIS OWN POCKET TO HELP STUDENTS ENROLL AT THE UNIVERSITY. SOMETIMES, WHEN THEY COULDN'T PAY THEIR DEBTS, HE WOULD ARRANGE FOR THEIR FAMILIES TO TRADE GOODS AND SERVICES IN EXCHANGE FOR TUITION — EVERYTHING FROM SHRUBBERY AND GRAVEL PARKING LOTS, TO REFRIGERATORS AND FOODSTUFFS.

GRANDPA'S INGENUITY IS CREDITED WITH HELPING THE UNIVERSITY SURVIVE THE DEPRESSION. IN HIS TWENTY-SEVEN YEAR CAREER, GRANDPA LOANED OUT A MILLION DOLLARS — ALL OF IT WAS REPAID.

WHEN B.B. AND JO WERE DRIVING OUT WEST ON THEIR HONEYMOON, THEY WANTED TO BE ALONE, BUT THEY PICKED UP A SIXTEEN-YEAR-OLD HITCHHIKER ON THEIR WAY BACK. THEY COULDN'T SHAKE HIM, AND HE RODE WITH THEM FOR OVER 500 MILES FROM YELLOWSTONE TO RAPID CITY. AT NIGHT THEY WOULD DROP HIM OFF, AND IN THE MORNING THEY WOULD FIND HIM ON THE ROAD WITH HIS THUMB OUT. ONE NIGHT THEY EVEN TUCKED HIM IN TO SLEEP. THE ENTIRE WAY THEY NEVER LET ON THAT THEY WERE ON THEIR HONEYMOON.

Pal Of My Heart,

If John and Mattie come along, I'm wondering what they would think of our demonstrations of affection in public? However, we can't afford to let the fact that there's someone along keep us from being on honeymoon. Then, too, if we've been married a month, maybe we'll be more or less "fed up" on affectionate demonstrations and it won't be as if we've just thrown off our wedding togs and started on our honeymoon. Now don't you understand me to mean that after a few months there'll be no petting parties at our house. If you don't continue to love me and demonstrate that affection, I'll break your neck, so beware!

Your very own,

JoJo

My Darling Jo,

So you are going to break my neck, are you? Well, that's fine. I just love a good tussle. However, you won't need to worry about my not showing my affection. It just pops out. I try to be more reserved and show my affection less, be more dignified, etc., but it just doesn't seem to come out that way. I know that even a blind man could see that I'm completely daffy about you. Even when I try to keep it dark. I've never been so completely happy as I have since you and I began our plans for a home together.

Your own Big Boy,

B.B.

Sweetheart O' Mine,

I've just spent twenty-five cents and two hours very profitably. I finished supper and decided on the spur of the moment to go to a movie at the Circle Theater. The picture was "The Adventures of Abraham Lincoln" and was a pictorial biography.

I wished for you many times as I watched the changing scenes of the picture. I wanted you terribly as I saw the love of Lincoln for Anne Rutledge, and I wished and wished to hold your hand as the picture moved to her death.

I was stirred by the martial music, the dashing cavalry, waving flags, and cheering populace even as were the youngsters who whistled and cheered as the pictures were shown. Yet I wanted so much that they might realize that that is not war, but only the allurement to war. My wish was answered in the next scene, when a Confederate captain shoots at a Union commander, who, starting to kill him, discovers it is his father, and his father dies in his arms, sobering the cheering audience.

Then as Lincoln walks through the graveyard at Gettysburg and observes a weeping mother, he turns to his aide and remarks, "There are the fruits of victory." I count this evening well spent too because it strips one of the excuse, "If I had a chance like so and so," for if anyone seemed to be less fortunate than Lincoln, it has passed my notice.

Sweetheart, I'm lonesome to have you with me to dream and talk and plan and work together. You are a big inspiration to me. All men cannot be President of the U.S.A., but all men can strive to deserve to be and you can help me do that at least. Now, at least, I would rather deserve to be and not be, than to be and not deserve to be.

Dearest, please accept the devotion of one who loves you with all his heart, and that one is,

       Your B.B.

Pal of My Heart,

You're just the man I've been dreaming of back in my subconscious mind all these years. I'm going to do my best not to disappoint my "Prince of Princes." I know, and so do you, the disadvantages of marrying as late in life as we shall, but our love and devotion, and our Father's help will insure our happiness against all these things. I'm certainly willing to go two-thirds of the way in making compromises and I'm sure you're willing to do as much. Instead of saying, "How much can I persuade him to give up?" I'll say, "How much can I give up for him?" I'm sure that with regards to major things, we shall be agreed, and the minor things matter so little.

I love my Big Boy more than I ever dreamed I could love any man,

JoJo

March 13, 1929 from Tulsa, Oklahoma

Darling JoJo,

When your letter came this morning, I had to tear the house down to get it. Doesn't that sound dramatic? A.L. took all the mail upstairs while I was waiting on a customer and attempted to toss your letter to me. It did not go straight but darted away, slipped down between the stairway and the window and under the stairway. I had to go in the front window, take out the glass, climb in under the stairway, then replace the glass and redecorate the window. However, it was worth all the effort.

Bushels of love and kisses from your,

Blakey

My Own Sweetheart,

You come from such a splendid family, and I think you deserve a wife who comes from such a family, and I fear you're not getting it. I talked things over with Adeline before I gave you my answer, because I wondered whether I ought to bring you into our family. Do you still love me, and do you still want me to be your life partner? Remember, you will be taking unto yourself one who comes from a family which is very ordinary. But you know how I love the church, and how interested I am in the higher things of life. I'm not boasting when I say that I have always lived a perfectly pure and upright life.

Bushels of love,

Jo

My Lovely Jo,

Do I still love you? You only succeed in making me love you more and more when you talk so foolishly.

Now don't you worry about me and your family. I fear you've placed a halo around my head and it doesn't belong there, for I'm far from being an angel. In fact, sometimes I think I am full of the very opposite.

Now, dear, it doesn't do any good for you to worry about things at home. When you and I see a chance to remedy any of these situations we will just roll up our mental, physical, and spiritual sleeves and pitch in. But until then you must just put your mind on the things you are doing.

Your future husband,

B.B. Blakey

Dearest of Sweethearts and My Own J.L.L.W.–PDQ,

Ha! Honey, what do those two L's stand for, and are you going to keep them all and mark the name J.L.L.W.B. when we are married? It's okay with me. I'm only curious.

Sweetheart, never for one least unit of time have I ever regretted that moment on the hill at Hollister when I asked you to be my wife. But each hour, it seems, my love for you has grown by leaps and bounds. Each letter and each hour of intimate acquaintance has shown me some new thing in your character and life to admire and love and cherish, and has made me more determined to make the most of my life in order that yours may be happier.

Your lover,

B.B.B.

March 19, 1929 from Ada, Oklahoma

My Own B.B.,

So you didn't know your girl already has four names? It's terrible to have such names imposed upon a baby. I think they thought I'd never have the opportunity to add the fourth name, so they gave it to me to make sure. Now this is how it happened. My father had an old flame after whom he chose to name me, and my mother was kind enough to give her consent. Well, the former girl's name was Josie; that was the first awful name they gave me. Mother had a sister and sister-in-law visiting us at the time, and they each asked that the second name be hers, so to keep from hurting their feelings, they gave me both names. Now, can you beat Josie Lou Lydia Walker for a name? Is it any wonder that I remain short? When I was only a small girl I began to dislike the name Josie and, when I was ready for the seventh grade, decided to go by Josephine. If you want to make me feel most awful, just call me that terrible name, Josie, and it will make me feel as good as to be called Rattlesnake or something.

Your girl loves you worlds,

Jo

IT SURPRISED ME TO READ THAT GRANDMA DISLIKED THE NAME JOSIE, BECAUSE THAT HAS BEEN HER NAME FOR AS LONG AS I CAN REMEMBER. WHEN HER CHILDREN DISCOVERED THAT HER NAME WAS NOT JOSEPHINE, BUT JOSIE LOU LYDIA, A NAME SHE DIDN'T PARTICULARLY LIKE, THEY BEGAN TO TEASE HER AND CALL HER BY HER TRUE NAME. EVENTUALLY, IT STUCK AND SHE DECIDED SHE LIKED IT AFTER ALL. SHE'S BEEN "JOSIE" EVER SINCE.

My Own Sweetheart,

There's always something new and unexpected coming up. This time, it happens that the church wants to keep me another three months. Please give me your advice. I'd love to remain settled a while longer. On the other hand, I already have a black eye from canceling my January field dates. I'm getting only $110 and my room here, while in the field I'd be getting $35 per week and all expenses paid. You understand, I'm sure, that the money does not make me want to get back into the field, except that I can better take care of my debts in that way, and can therefore hasten our wedding.

Oodles of love,

Jo

During her career, Grandma wrote many religious education materials, including children's stories. When I was growing up, my favorite bedtime stories were the ones my Grandma told me. They weren't in books, but they were original and there was always a moral to the story.

Sweetheart O' Mine,

I've decided finally to go on to Kentucky. It would certainly be unfair to Kentucky to turn them down at this late date. The people in Ada have known all the time that I was contracted to stay only till Easter. Why didn't they move faster? I've thought and prayed about this matter and my conscience tells me not to cancel my dates. These churches in Kentucky have asked for me.

I love my Big Boy,

J.L.L.W.

Dearest JoJo,

I can only congratulate myself upon having selected a life partner who thinks of what is right more than her own wishes. I wish you might have stayed in Ada, but under the circumstances I quite agree with your decision. You make me love you more and more every day as you confirm my opinion of your loveliness. I am so proud of the work you are doing that I want to tell everyone about it. I think my girl is just wonderful.

Your own lover,

B.B. Blakey

Darling O' Mine,

I thought that sometime we would have a home that would radiate the desire to learn and the spirit of study. Not cramming for an exam, but of contact with the higher things. I should like for that home to be accessible to young people who now are not given the vision of their own possibilities, and through that experience they will desire to make the most of their lives, in service, and be led to a greater vision of their possibilities.

Your lover,

B.B.B.

WHEN MY MOM WAS GROWING UP, HER FAMILY HAD THE ONLY SET OF ENCYCLOPEDIAS IN THEIR NEIGHBORHOOD, SO EVERYONE CAME OVER TO DO HOMEWORK AT THEIR HOUSE. GRANDPA WOULD READ THOSE ENCYCLOPEDIAS LIKE A BOOK. AS HE WENT ALONG, HE WOULD CROSS-REFERENCE INFORMATION UNTIL HE HAD A CARD TABLE FULL OF OPEN BOOKS.

THROUGHOUT HIS CHILDREN'S HIGH SCHOOL AND COLLEGE YEARS, HE WOULD PICK UP THEIR TEXTBOOKS AND QUIZ EVERYONE AT THE DINNER TABLE. HE EVEN TRIED TO TEACH HIMSELF TO READ FRENCH IN ORDER TO KEEP UP ON WHAT ONE OF HIS CHILDREN WAS LEARNING.

Pal O' Mine,

You couldn't in a year guess why I'm so worn out. I'll bet I've walked three miles hunting a white georgette dress. Can you guess what I want with it? You're right, I want it to wear on that day of supreme happiness, when we shall pledge ourselves to each other. I've decided that each thing which I shall wear on that day will have been purchased in a different town. Am getting my dress with the idea in mind that it can be worn after the wedding. How's that for practical?

Love,

> *Jo*

My Sweetheart,

You poor little motherless boy. I know it must have been hard and tedious to make repairs on your coat lining! I'm sorry that your girl wasn't there to do it for you. It won't be long now till I shall do all such things for you. I'm not very good at it myself, but am sure that my fingers will work better than yours.

I'm having a hard time trying to be alone. The town is full of folks who are attending the horse races, and all hotels are full, so there is constantly someone calling or coming for rooms here at the Y. There are three persons in this room, and almost every night one moves on and another comes in.

The girls all think I have a mighty good-looking Sweetie. They've all been raving about your picture.

Oodles of love to my neglected Big Boy,

> *Your own JoJo*

Dearest of Sweethearts,

Sweetheart, it surely warmed my heart for you to tell me of that errand that took so much of your time. Now I must ask Frances what a georgette dress is. See how my education has been neglected?

Now what should I wear? Overalls or a dress suit? Now remember that I'm depending on you to steer me right so that I won't make any blunders.

By some miracle I have no formal duties tomorrow evening. How I wish that I were to spend it with my sweetheart just reading, discussing, enjoying, and reveling in our freedom.

Sometimes I feel as though I were a production machine, producing hardware service, religious education, etc. and not consuming. I just want to learn for the thrill of understanding, to see for the thrill that comes from seeing, to just consume, take in, absorb, travel, be irresponsible, carefree, forget time, appointments, cooperations, dependence of others, and do nothing as long and as often as it pleases me. Yet reason tells me that unless I perform some service to make someone else happy, better, more contented or their life easier, that it would all turn to dust and ashes and I should be miserable.

I love you, dear. Come let me work for you.

Your own Bernard

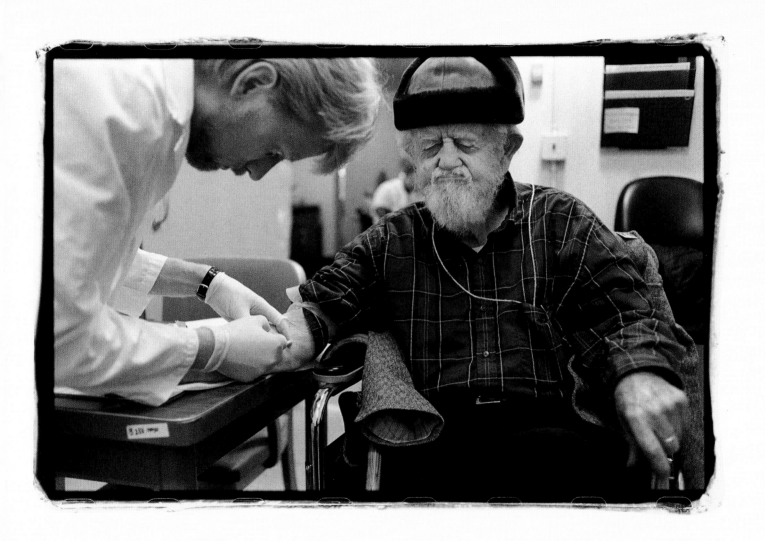

My Sweet Big Boy,

Honey, I dream of the joy which will be ours as we begin our home together. I know you will enjoy making a garden and so will I, but sweetheart, when in the world will you have any time? Will it always be necessary for you to work twelve hours a day at the store? That will mean we can't have our evening meal before seven. Of course, I can do some of those things while you're at the store, but it won't be half as much fun. I've had in mind, too, that I'd like for us to have a friendship flower garden, one off to itself and one in which we plant only favorite flowers given us by good friends. How does that strike you?

Worlds of love and kisses, from your very own,

Jo

May 3, 1929 from Tulsa, Oklahoma

My Partner,

When will I have any time to work in the garden? Well dear! I work from the time I get up until midnight most every day. If it isn't work at the store it is church work, and of course it is a great joy. I do not feel that it is drudgery. I'll simply turn over a part of the church work that I do at night to you to do during the day, so that we can work together on our home and garden. Now don't you think I'm a schemer?

I'm usually pretty prompt and will close the store at 7:00, be home at 7:10, washed up in five minutes, and we'll sit down to eat exactly (ahem) at 7:15. It takes me just twenty minutes to eat, and at 7:40 it is still light. Then, in the summertime we will be industriously working in the garden. We will have radishes and lettuce and peas and beans, a good strawberry bed, tomatoes, sweet potatoes and onions, of course. Do you know how to can fruits and vegetables?

Your very own,

Blakey

"MY WHAT A DREADFUL COLD! ... STAYED IN BED ALL DAY EXCEPT LONG ENOUGH TO GO DOWN AND EAT DINNER ... CAME BACK UP HERE TO WRITE TO MY SWEETIE WHEN HERE COME A BOX OF LOVELY CARNATIONS FROM HIM! FIFTEEN PERFECT BEAUTIES! I'D LIKE TO SQUEEZE HIM TO PIECES SOMETIMES ..."

... FROM JO'S DIARY, JANUARY 31, 1929

My Adorable Jo,

Eleven years ago next July 14, I was in France on the Marne River. The Germans selected that day to make their last drive toward Paris through our sector, and so that day marks the beginning of the greatest battle in which I participated. So, I suppose that it would be a good day for us to start ours. (Don't you think so? Ha!) I want you to note that I left it to you to decide whether we fight shoulder to shoulder or face to face. Personally, I have a decided preference.

This date would give us about ten days at home before starting west. That is allowing two weeks to go and one to return. Another thing that causes me to prefer the 14th to the 21st is that it is a whole week sooner, and that last week of waiting already seems like a year. May we not set the date as July 14th, dear?

If we do not have a church wedding, or a big one, will it be necessary for me to have a best man? Should I have a best man? You see, I'm as ignorant as can be, for I've never been through this before. Ha!

Even if we do not invite guests, I would like to be married in a church since it can't be in Shirleys' home. It will just seem more reverent and binding than in a strange home.

Darling, I'm in the seventh heaven of delight and ecstasy at our troth and plans. I'm just like a little boy with his first party and can hardly wait until the day arrives.

Oodles of love and kisses from,

Your Big Boy

GRANDPA ATTRIBUTED THE SUCCESS OF THEIR LONG MARRIAGE TO "THE FACT THAT WE TALK. I TELL HER AT LEAST TWICE EVERY DAY THAT I LOVE HER. CONVERSATION PASSES IDEAS ACROSS AND PEOPLE OUGHT TO TALK. WHEN WE HAVE A DISAGREEMENT WE SOLVE IT WITH A TALK-A-THON."

My Fine Big Boy,

I'm just as joyful as you are most of the time. I'll have to confess that once in a while I wonder if I've weighed all things properly. They say love is blind, and I guess that's right. I'm sure we both realize that there will be many hard adjustments to be made and that each of us has many settled ideas which won't be easy to adjust in order to become congenial. But honey, the hardest thing of all will be <u>just getting used to each other.</u> I feel that we are at a great disadvantage because we do not know each other as we should. We think we know each other, but <u>how can we really</u>, when we've actually been together only a few hours at a time and just a few times? I trust we can be alone much of the time during the first six weeks of our married life. I'm glad we're going west, for that will help lots.

I know you must think me very foolish, and no doubt you didn't know I felt this way. Had our courtship been more normal, we could have learned to know wherein each is sensitive. Maybe I'd better tell you that I am easily embarrassed. All my life I've tried to break myself of blushing at most anything, but am still that way. I'm sure many folk would be greatly surprised to learn how very much I dread going into a new place and having to meet new people. After three years' constant travel, I'm still sensitive about it.

Love,

Jo

When Grandma and Grandpa finished researching their family histories, they settled in Minnesota to be near their only grandchildren. They built a new home on the banks of the Mississippi near Little Falls (which Grandpa insisted on roofing himself, at age seventy-five). Later, when Mom took a job in the Twin Cities, they moved to a nearby condominium in downtown Minneapolis.

My Own True Love,

The special delivery letter was just as sweet as can be. You seem to understand even my innermost thoughts. I'm just as certain of our happiness as I would be were we already married. We're interested in the same things and we love each other. I think your idea of selecting a secret place for us to stay during the few days in Tulsa before going west, is a capital suggestion.

I had a sweet letter from my mother, in which she <u>tried</u> to tell me how much your letter meant to her. She has tried to answer it, but she fears her answer will not be intelligible to you. It takes practice to get on to her particular style, but I know you will appreciate the answer. Mother was permitted to go to school only until she was in eighth grade. She's the sweetest mother on earth and I know you will love her. She says every member of our family has read your letter and they all think it is mighty fine.

Will I trust my Big Boy? Will I love him? Will I expect great things of him? Why, a thousand times yes!!! I'll do this or I'll shoot him. If I shoot, I'll use Cupid's arrows.

Can you not see that the train is moving? Do you realize that this trip practically ends my career as a gadabout? I'm not sorry.

I love you heaps,

Jo

Darling Jo,

We did not get to talk very much about the details of our wedding, did we, dear? Either way you suggested about announcements is satisfactory with me. I do not understand just what obligations in the way of expense either would entail. I'm woefully ignorant of wedding etiquette.

Honey, I just do not have words to express the joy I have in you, your high ideals, your sympathetic, understanding nature, your cheery smile, your energy, conversation, perseverance. I love you because you are just you.

Your own,

B.B.

My Own B.B.,

Thanks, honey, for sending the names and addresses of your family. I'll be writing them about our plans. I want you to send me the names of everyone to whom you wish to send announcements. Relative to expenses, you will want to be responsible for the following: the clergyman's fee, my bouquet, my wedding ring (of course), the license (of course), and I think that's all. I'll be responsible for everything else. If I were you, I'd weigh this thing pretty heavily to see if it will be worth all these things! Ha! Maybe we'd better arrange to get the rings in Enid so as to get them alike.

The news of my wedding is spreading already. Miss Goddard started it. We don't care, do we?

Must write to Mother. Bushels of love,

Jo

GRANDPA LOST HIS WEDDING RING EARLY IN THE MARRIAGE AND IT WASN'T REPLACED UNTIL THEIR SIXTIETH ANNIVERSARY, WHEN THE CHILDREN GAVE HIM A NEW ONE.

IN THE 1960s, MUCH TO EVERYONE'S CHAGRIN, GRANDMA REPLACED HER ORIGINAL BASKET-STYLE ENGAGEMENT RING WITH A MORE MODERN SOLITAIRE-STYLE RING.

My Own Darling,

Now, about weighing this proposition to see if it will be worth the expense. There might be ways to keep the expense down to where it <u>would</u> be worth it. Everyone gets flowers from the Shirleys' garden, so I could pick the bouquet there. We used to make rings from horseshoe nails and we have plenty of those at the store. Perhaps I could pick up a second-hand license somewhere, since there are so many divorces these days, and they say that when you ask the preacher how much it comes to, he usually leaves it to the groom, or else tells you that the law allows him three dollars and you can give him fifty cents and say, "Well, this makes it three-fifty." Ha! Under these circumstances, I believe I could afford it. Ha! I'll be so glad to get you. I'll feel like giving the preacher all I've got and maybe I'm cheating him then.

Be sure and tell me whether I should arrange for a best man. That is one sad part about a wedding. The bride never gets the best man.

Your lover,

B.B.

My Sweetheart Pal,

I have not been planning to use a bridesmaid, so you need not use a best man. I'll have the <u>best</u> man at my side. Remember you must come to Enid to get the license, it must be gotten in the county in which the marriage is performed. Don't feel too badly about <u>all</u> this expense! I <u>told</u> you you didn't know what you were bargaining for. Ha! Remember, you said you'd be married only once, and we're to be married a long, long, time I trust. So it ought to be worth much more than either of us will pay. And I fear Shirleys' roses will be gone. Ha!

Well, consolations to my frugal laddie!

I love him with all my heart.

Jo

Light of My Life,

Eleven years ago today, I lay around a stable in France with everything I possessed rolled up in a pack and ready to leave for the front at a moment's notice. All we did all day long was to sit and think and grouch at one another until after suppertime, when the bugle blew "Assembly" and the command came, "Fall in," and there was a mad scramble to get our packs on our backs and our places in line, and the column swung down the road to our train of boxcars and we began to sing, "Where Do We Go From Here, Boys." So we started for our first scrap.

Tonight, we four Blakeys went to the Ritz to see Mary Pickford in "The Coquette." It is a tragic picture, well played. When they embraced, I could almost imagine I felt your warm, soft arms steal around my neck, feel them tighten and hold me firm and strong as if to say, "Isn't it a joy that we belong each to the other?"

I got my car, took your letter downtown to mail it and straightened out my dresser drawer. Sorted out your letters to me according to date and reread some. Especially one written October 10 that said, "Does this sound like I love you?"

Your devoted,

Blakey

My Darling Jo,

Sweetheart, our wedding day is one day nearer. We will have heaps of fun selecting the patterns of china, silverware, color schemes, furniture and then figuring out a way to buy and pay for them.

Your own,

B.B.

Pal O' Mine,

My, aren't you the stingy thing with your kisses! To think that I could get enough in one short visit to last me for a whole month. Yes, I know they are sweet, but you haven't gauged my appetite correctly. Remember what Sister Susan said about your "affectionate lover." I surely am. I'll need a lot of kisses, so be sure to keep a huge supply on hand for all the time after we are married. I guess I'm just starved for affection.

Good night, dear, I love you.

B.B.

My Own Darling,

Honey, your love for children is equaled only by mine and endears you to my heart. Sometimes I wish you and I might be relieved of the responsibilities to older folk and just become children together with other children, and lead them as we wish we might have been led, as we look back at the mistakes we each have made in life.

I'm longing for the time when you and I shall confer and work together. Your experience and training are greater than mine and I shall defer to your judgment most of the time, for I have great respect for its worth and I say this with no thought of any inferiority complex either.

I love you,

B.B.B.

My Own Darling Jo,

One month from now we'll be kneeling side by side answering the most important questions of our lives and promising to love, honor, cherish, (and will you promise to obey? Ha!).

I am your own,

B.B.B.

IN 1932 THE HUSBAND OF JO'S OLDER
SISTER EMMA DIED, LEAVING HER A
WIDOW WITH THREE CHILDREN. B.B.
AND JO INVITED HER DAUGHTER FLOY,
AGE FOURTEEN, TO COME TO TULSA AND
SPEND THE SUMMER. SHE STAYED WITH
THEM FOR TEN YEARS, FINISHING HIGH
SCHOOL AND TWO YEARS OF COLLEGE,
BEFORE MARRYING IN 1942.

June 18, 1929 from Tulsa, Oklahoma

My Wife To Be,

I hope that God will bless our union with the sunshine that children bring to the home. Should that not be the case, dear, though I feel sure it will, still we can give some homeless children the advantages of a Christian home and bless our own lives by the joys which they bring.

Your loving,

B.B.

June 18, 1929 from Fairview, Oklahoma · Tuesday evening

Dearest B.B.,

Mr. Malone tells me to tell you not to let me run over you. I told Mr. M. not to worry for I wouldn't have a husband whom I could run over. But now listen, young man, neither would I have one who would run over me, so beware!

I'm too sleepy to finish this. Honey, I'll try not to be tired and sleepy when we're married.

Bushels of love to my own Romeo from your,

JoJo

June 19, 1929 from Tulsa, Oklahoma

My Darling Jo,

Cousin Will Buckner died yesterday at age 101. Shall we live together to be that old, dear?

Heaps of love,

B.B.

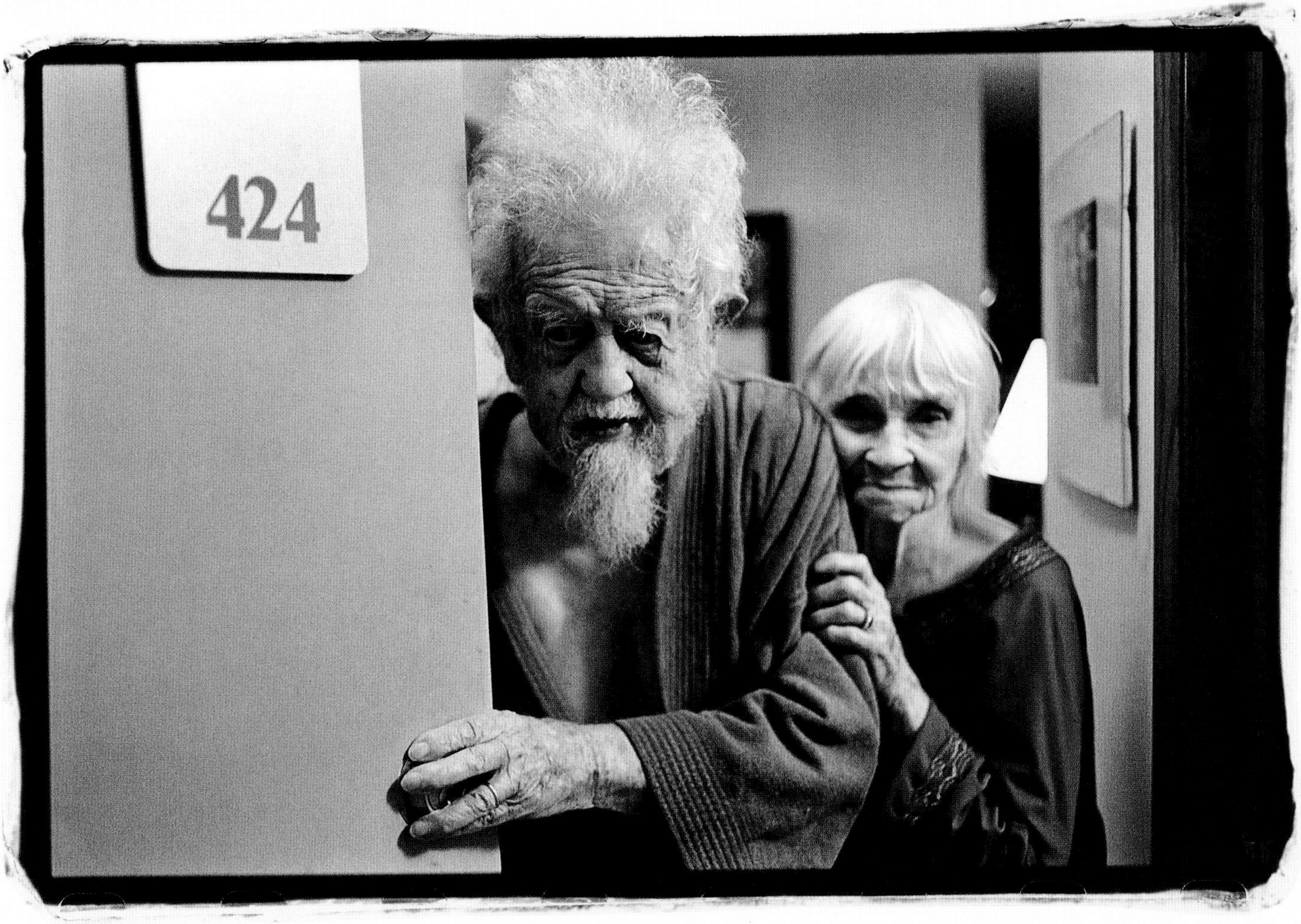
424

My Own Lovely Lady,

Sometimes I wonder, dear, why we are put in this world. Is this life a preparation for one to come? The emphasis being on the preparation, because I do not doubt the one to come. Is it a testing place? I wish I knew just what God's purpose is for me.

Do not think I'm downhearted because I talk like this, for I'm not. I could not talk to anyone else in this way in a million years. It is just that you seem so much a part of me that it seems I must dream and think with you. Do you mind?

Your own,

B.B.

My Lonely Big Boy,

Miss Goddard has dated me as promised for three schools this fall. I told her she could count on me. I still have a $75 debt hanging over me. Had planned to cut it down to $50, but found it necessary to do some repair work on our house and to do some other things for my family. And sweetheart, it simply costs a great deal to make preparations to get married, even though no elaborate preparations are being made. But I'm not sorry, for it's worth a million times more. Just think of the happiness which is beckoning to us. And when these things are shared with one who cares and loves, the joy will be doubled. Oh, I know there'll be some heartaches but with one like my Big Boy, they won't be hard to bear. You can count on Jo to do as much for you as you will do for her, for "Love suffers long and is kind."

Bushels of love,

JoJo

GRANDMA HAS RETAINED HER POSITIVE ATTITUDE DESPITE THE DECAY OF SHORT-TERM MEMORY. ONE DAY, WHEN MY MOM WAS DROPPING MY GRAND-PARENTS OFF AFTER A LONG AFTERNOON OF TESTS AT THE CLINIC, GRANDMA GOT OUT OF THE CAR AND SAID, WITH A SMILE, "WELL, I DON'T REMEMBER WHERE WE'VE BEEN BUT IT'S BEEN A LOVELY AFTERNOON."

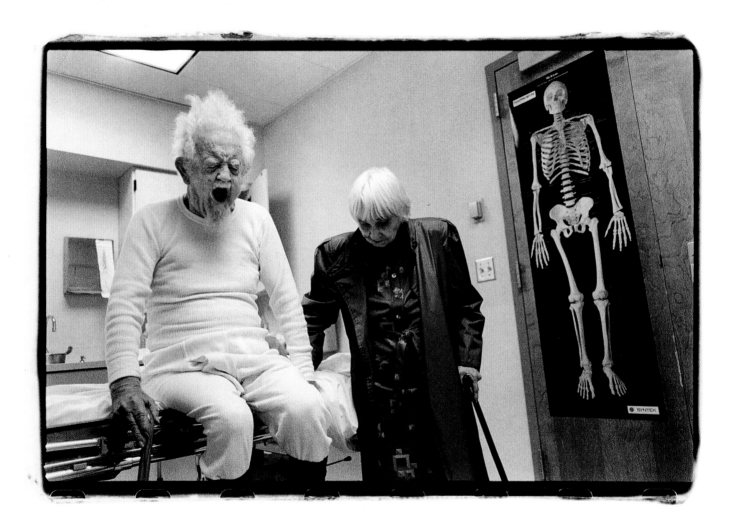

My Own Prince Charming,

Honey Boy, there's one very important matter which we have never discussed but relative to which I think we should come to a definite understanding. I think I realize how very eager you are that we shall have children. I'm sure you realize also that it would just about break my heart if we could not. I, too, have absolute faith that God will grant us that privilege. But sweetheart, I think it would be wise to take precautions so that we may have time to get acquainted with each other before we must engage in the delightful preparation for "the little bit of heaven" which we trust God will send to make our home complete. I'm sure that a girl cannot be quite herself during such a time, and I do trust that we may have time to enjoy "just ourselves" for a time. If you haven't already informed yourself about this matter, I wish you would, and I'll do the same. Perhaps you have reliable information at hand. If not, I'm sure you can receive help from a physician.

I love you with all my heart,

Jo

"I've spent most of the morning reading *Youth and Sex* by Kirby Page. It was very helpful."

... from Jo's diary, July 4, 1929

Roy was born a year after their marriage and Marian was born three years later. My mom, B.J., was Grandma's "menopause baby," born three years after Marian. Grandma had her first two children in the hospital. After that she figured she knew how to do it, and she gave birth to my mom at home in Enid, Oklahoma.

94

Darling JoJo,

Your two good letters have filled me with more happiness than I know how to tell you about. What you say of a feeling of peace, rest, etc. makes me love you more and more, and fills me with assurance that our life together will be all that it should be and with resolve to do my share to make it so. And what you say about "the little bit of heaven" so exactly describes my sentiments and desires that you fill me with indescribable happiness. Remember during this last week that there is one who holds you dearer than life itself, and loves you with an abiding love, and that one is your own Big Boy,

Bernard

Pal O' My Dreams,

This will be the last letter I shall be writing to my sweetheart for a while. As you drive to Wichita, keep in mind that I love you with all my heart. Honey, don't be too free with your demonstrations of affections while we're here. There'll be plenty of occasions afterward.

JoJo

In order to respect her mother's wishes, Grandma moved the wedding from Enid to her home church in Wichita, Kansas.

My Own Darling Jo,

I believe this is the last letter you will receive from me before you change your name to Mrs. B.B. Blakey. What a happy thought it is that I shall see you very soon and that we need not be parted again for any length of time. The future looks bright and shining and my heart is overflowing with happiness.

All my love is yours, dear,

Bernard

"ABOUT 8:00 A.M. I WENT OVER TO ANNA MAE JONES' TO GET THE BASKET WHICH MARY ELIZABETH WAS TO CARRY. MARY B. CAME ABOUT 9:30 AND DECORATED THE BASKET WHILE BESS HELPED ME TO GET DRESSED. MY ROMEO CAME ABOUT 11:00, ALL SPRUCED UP.

"WE TOOK H.O., MARY, AND EMMA WITH US TO THE CHURCH. IT WAS A BEASTLY HOT DAY, BUT THE HOUSE WAS PACKED. BROTHER THORNTON PREACHED A LONG SERMON ON THE SUBJECT 'ONIONS AND GARLIC.'

"Before the ceremony, Mary sang 'I Love You Truly.' Everyone said she sang 'so sweetly.' Marjorie K. played Lohengrin's Wedding March as we marched down the west aisle.

"The service went off perfectly, Brother Thornton being the only one who was in the least nervous."

… from Jo's diary, July 14, 1929

EPILOGUE

GRANDPA. I MISS YOU SO MUCH. WHEN I
HUGGED YOU, I FELT ALL YOUR VULNERABILITY
AND ALL YOUR STRENGTH AT THE SAME TIME.
I FELT THE WISDOM OF YOUR NINETY-SEVEN
YEARS, AND I FELT THE LITTLE BOY WHO WAS
DEPENDENT ON OTHERS FOR HIS SURVIVAL.

On the night of his ninety-seventh birthday, Grandma called to say that Grandpa was lying on the bathroom floor. Mom and I rushed over; I knew it was the beginning of the end. We called the paramedics and Grandma kissed Grandpa goodbye before they wheeled him off to the emergency room. I went with the ambulance and Mom took care of Grandma.

While in the emergency room, Grandpa had a seizure. I grabbed him and talked into his ear, telling how much I loved him, and that if he really wanted to leave, he could, but that I really wanted him to stay. Suddenly, he started to breathe again. He came back with all the clarity that he had had before. He told me how special his wife was, and that there was no one nicer or better in the whole world. I said, "And next to her is you," and he said, "Next to nobody."

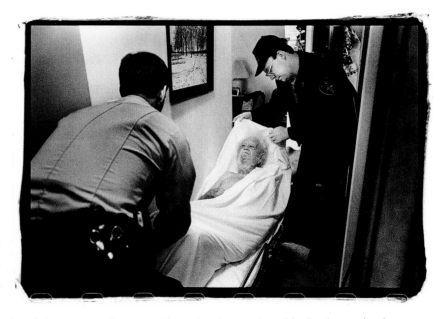

The doctor asked B.B. if he wanted to be resuscitated if he should start to go. Grandpa said, "Growing old is terrible but the alternative is worse." He told the doctor that he wanted to live. He said that his other granddaughter had been living in Italy and now was in Washington, D.C., and that he wanted to be around for her visit.

The hospital set up a daybed for me right next to his bed and during one of our very short sleeping sessions, I had a dream that he went "code blue," which is what happens when someone is dying.

Grandpa's blood pressure continued to climb and, although his voice was not strong and sure, he seemed normal. He remembered the names of his nurses, and he spent an hour telling a doctor stories about how he won his part of World War I, in the battle of the Marne, for which he was awarded a Silver Star. I talked on the phone with family members and we all felt pretty sure that he was doing well.

Around five, I started asking him if I could turn on the TV to watch the national news and he said, "No, I like it quiet. Your grandmother is always wanting to have the TV on and I let her, because love means putting the needs of your beloved ahead of your own — constantly. But I don't like it." At a few minutes before five-thirty he said, "Okay, you can have the TV on for half an hour." Just as the news came on, Mom called to say that she and Grandma were getting ready to come over to the hospital. Then Grandpa said he wanted to have his bed lowered so he could be lying down, "all the way down."

I lowered the electric hospital bed, and he turned on his side and started to blow short, quick breaths. I looked at the monitor to see his heart rate go up; I pushed the button for the nurse and yelled for help. The hospital staff went into "code blue." After fifteen minutes, a doctor came out and brought me into a room to tell me Grandpa was gone.

The pain that remains goes as deep as the roots that Grandpa worked so hard to uncover in our family. He cared about history. Not only his own, but for the hundreds of people who were kin to him, and the history of the world. He was a source of inspiration for conversation, just as much as his lapsing into the same old story was a conversation stopper. He wasn't afraid to interject a heavy theoretical question into a light meal. He was very stubborn, and being dependent on others was very difficult for him.

Grandma never got to see Grandpa again, but he is never far from her mind. Her constant refrain is, "Bless his heart, he was the nicest person I ever knew." After a lot of anguish, our family decided that Grandma should move to the First Christian Church Residence that is connected to her church community. Everyone thought that she would die of a broken heart without her husband, but she has remained in good health and has kept her cheerful nature and quick wit.

At age ninety-eight, following a couple of falls, she now walks with a walker, but she loves to say, "I don't mind because I was a Walker for thirty-two years." Her short-term memory is nonexistent, but her recollection of the past is astounding. When going through the courtship letters, I would lie in bed with her and she would tell me about the people in the stories, and her mind would be as clear as a bell. Then, in her positive way, she would ask me again to read her the letters.

I am so lucky to have had such a long, intimate relationship with my grandparents. They have shaped my outlook on life. I am happy to have this opportunity to share their story with others who are interested in long-lasting love, and growing old with the person you love. I have included the end of their love story to acknowledge the nature of impermanence in life, but I feel that the legacy of their vision of love will live on, long after their time on earth has passed.

My True Love,

For some time I've known that I love you, but of late, the last week or so, it seems that I have a different feeling, a greater feeling of peace, rest, protection, absolute trust and devotion to you. I have no fear of anything in connection with our life together, and feel that I could be content anywhere, and do anything for you. I feel that life would be empty without you. A feeling of horror comes over me when I even think of losing you. You are in my thoughts as I journey into dreamland each night, and when I open my eyes each morning, I find myself offering a silent prayer for your protection. I wish I could tell you how much you mean to me.

I love you with all my heart,

Your own JoJo

THIS BOOK IS MY FAMILY AND MY LIFE

AS MY GRANDMA SAYS, "I'M HAPPY, NOT FOR MYSELF, BUT BECAUSE THE BOOK MIGHT HELP SOMEBODY, AND ALL I'VE EVER WANTED TO DO IS BE OF HELP."

Many thanks to B.J. French (my wonderful editor-mom), her husband John, my sister Kimberly Mahling Clark, my Aunt Marian Spencer and my Uncle Roy Blakey, my Grandma, Grandpa, and my late father's now-deceased parents, Henry and Birdie Pickett, who are my small immediate family. I want to honor my extended family, the Mahlings, and my family of choice, Michal Daniel (my life-partner) and his son Stephen, and my friends. They all constantly challenge and help me in exploring key life issues, making life interesting and fun.

Photography provides a framework for thinking about the world. It is a medium that moves me to explore what is meaningful for me in life. Photographer Mary Ellen Mark helped me by encouraging me to make more photos of my grandparents. In 1983, Fred McDarrah gave me my start as a professional photographer in New York at *The Village Voice* newspaper. My wonderful colleagues at *People* magazine continue to provide me with a bridge into the lives of others. Thanks also to Abby Heyman, Mary Virginia Swanson, Margaret Wurtele, Cal Litsey, and Justine Charles for their early encouragement and advice. I am also grateful to Gary Chassman for his vision of the book and to Robert Yerks for translating that vision so beautifully in his design.

I have photographed family life, kids coping with life-threatening illness, people in the later stages of AIDS, my friends in the Native American and Tibetan communities, and my family. A thank-you to all those who opened their doors to me and who so selflessly give us all a glimpse of their lives through my camera.

Many arts organizations and foundations have contributed to my financial ability to develop my work as an artist: the Jerome Foundation, the McKnight Foundation, the Bush Foundation, and the National Endowment for the Arts. Thanks to Jon Oulman for exhibiting this work in his gallery.

A number of magazines helped me share my grandparents' story along the way, including *Life*, *The Village Voice*, *Mpls/St. Paul*, the *Utne Reader*, and *Stern* and *Frau Bilder* in Germany.

Keri Pickett

The Photographs

The contemporary photographs were created with my assorted Nikon cameras and my Leica M6 camera on Kodak TX3200 and TX400 film. All the recent images were shot in Minneapolis, Minnesota.